moja means one

moja means one

SWAHILI COUNTING BOOK

by Muriel Feelings · pictures by Tom Feelings

A PUFFIN PIED PIPER

First Pied Piper Printing 1976
Printed in Hong Kong by Wing King Tong Company Ltd.
20 19 18 17 16
MOJA MEANS ONE is published in a hardcover edition by
Dial Books for Young Readers,
375 Hudson Street, New York, New York 10014
ISBN 0-14-054662-6

To all Black children living
in the Western Hemisphere,
hoping you will one day
speak the language—in Africa

the continent of Africa, showing countries where Swahili is spoken

CONGO

ZAIRE

UGANDA
Kampala ★

KENYA

SOMALIA

★ Mogadishu

★ Nairobi

RWANDA
Kigali ★

Bujumbura ★
BURUNDI

+ MT. KILIMANJARO

Brazzaville ★

★ Kinshasa

TANZANIA

★ Dar es Salaam

Z A M B I A

MALAWI

MOZAMBIQUE

Lusaka ★

Zomba ★

MALAGASY REPUBLIC

★ Tananarive

★ Lourenço Marques

NILE

RIVER

introduction

All over the world people speak different languages. Languages differ according to the country or society in which people live. People use numbers for counting, and the words for numbers are from the words of their language. You may know some words from languages other than English, but do you know any words from an African language?

Africa, one of the largest continents in the world, spreads over 11 million square miles. There are about 800 African languages spoken in the many nations of this vast continent. Swahili is spoken across a wider geographical area than any other single language. It is the language of about 45 million people in the eastern part of Africa: in Kenya, Uganda, two-fifths of Zaire, on the coasts of Mozambique and Somalia, in the northern part of Malawi and Zambia, and by the townspeople of Rwanda, Burundi, and in Rhodesia as a language of commerce. It is spoken on the islands off the coast of East Africa such as Seychelles, Kilwa, and the Malagasy Republic. It is the national language of Tanzania. A person from Zaire can speak with a person of Kenya, a Tanzanian can talk with a Ugandan or Rwandan. One major importance of learning Swahili is that it serves as a common language and a unifying force among the many varying cultures and countries of Africa.

I lived for two years in Uganda and taught in a high school in Kampala, the capital. I also had the opportunity to travel around Uganda, to parts of Kenya, Tanzania, and Zaire, visiting with families in cities and villages throughout the countryside. Though the people in each country were of various ethnic groups and spoke their own language, they also spoke Swahili. Therefore I could communicate with them, though my knowledge of Swahili was limited. I found that in learning this language, I understood more of the culture (the way of life, the customs, values, history) of my people in East Africa.

Africa is the original homeland of about 100 million Black people who live in the United States, Canada, Central and South America, and the Caribbean islands. As our people in the Western Hemisphere learn more and more about our African heritage, we become increasingly proud. Part of our heritage is language. For example, in various Black communities in the United States, many of our people have taken Swahili names, Black students are learning Swahili in schools and colleges, private schools and shops bear Swahili names such as *Uhuru Sasa* (Freedom Now) School and *Uhuru Kitabu* (Freedom Book) Shop.

I have written this book in the hope that young boys and girls of African origin will enjoy learning to count in Swahili, together with gaining more knowledge of their African heritage.

Muriel Feelings

—

moja means one

1 moja
(mo·jah)

Snowy Kilimanjaro is the highest mountain in Africa.

2 mbili
(m·bee·lee)

Mankala, a counting game, is played by villagers young and old.

3 tatu
(ta·too)

Farmers grow **coffee trees** in all parts of East Africa.

4 nne
(n·nay)

Mothers usually carry their babies on their backs while walking.

5 tano
(tah·no)

Many kinds of animals roam the grassy savannah lands.

6 sita
(see·tah)

The **clothing** East Africans wear includes the kanga, busuti, lapa, kanzu, and dashiki.

7 saba
(sah·bah)

The Nile River, which flows between Uganda and Egypt, is filled with fish.

8 nane
(nah·nay)

Busy **market stalls** are stocked with fruits, vegetables, meats, fish, clothes, jewelry, pottery, and carvings.

9 tisa
(tee·sah)

Men play drums, thumb pianos, bamboo flutes, and other instruments.

10 kumi
(koo·mee)

At night in villages old people tell stories to **children** around the fireside.

AUTHOR'S NOTE

Kiswahili is the proper name for the language we call Swahili. The prefix *ki* denotes the actual language rather than the people who speak the language. (For example, a person who speaks Swahili would refer to the language spoken by the Ganda people as "kiganda," and to the Luo language as "kiluo.")

Because city life is basically similar around the world, I have not discussed it in this book. My intent rather has been to acquaint readers with what is unique about East African life. It is important, however, that children also learn about African cities, governments, universities, commerce, the arts, and other aspects of African culture.

MURIEL FEELINGS was born in Philadelphia, Pennsylvania, and attended California State College. She has lived in Guyana, South America, and in East Africa, where she taught for two years. Upon her return to the United States she taught high-school art in Brooklyn, New York. Her book *Jambo Means Hello: Swahili Alphabet Book* (Dial and Puffin Pied Piper), the companion to *Moja Means One*, was also illustrated by Tom Feelings and was a Caldecott Honor Book, an ALA Notable, and a Child Study Association Book of the Year. Ms. Feelings currently lives in Philadelphia.

TOM FEELINGS, well-known illustrator and artist, was born in Brooklyn, New York, and attended the School of Visual Arts. In 1971 Mr. Feelings became the first African-American artist to win a Caldecott Honor with his illustrations for *Moja Means One* (Dial and Puffin Pied Piper). Among the other award-winning books he has illustrated are *To Be a Slave*, a Newbery Honor Book by Julius Lester, and most recently the Coretta Scott King Award winner *Soul Looks Back in Wonder* (both Dial), a celebration of African-American creativity for which such distinguished writers as Maya Angelou, Margaret Walker, and Walter Dean Myers wrote poems. Mr. Feelings is a professor of art at the University of South Carolina in Columbia, South Carolina.